JONAH

The Reluctant Preacher

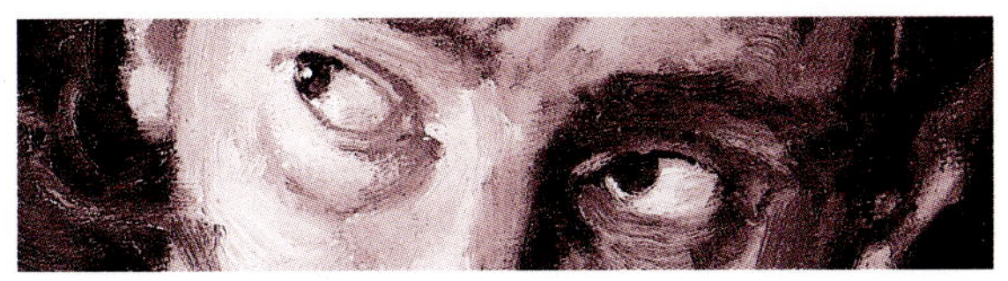

John A. Miller

NORTHWESTERN PUBLISHING HOUSE
Milwaukee, Wisconsin

To God's great blessings in my life:

My wife, Kristen, who has lovingly kept this prophet from the depths.
My son, J.J., who continually makes me proud.
My parents, John and LaVerne, who have given so much.
And God's people, in whose lives I have seen his Word work.

Cover illustration: Johnson and Fancher
Interior illustrations: Troy Allen, Samantha Burton, Frank Ordaz

Northwestern Publishing House
1250 N. 113th St., Milwaukee, WI 53226-3284
www.nph.net

Published 2004
Printed in the United States of America
ISBN 0-8100-1342-8

CONTENTS

FOREWORD

They have been referred to as the saints, the Hebrews, the Israelites, a remnant, and the church. They are God's people—his *chosen* people. They belong to him; so precious that he would go to impossible lengths to overcome the gulf that separates them from himself. You and I are among them.

The books in this series are a recital of the life and times of some of them—Noah, Jacob, Ruth, David, Jonah, Paul, and others. Their stories involve conflict and resolution, pain and tragedy, despondency and renewal. They present disturbing images from the underbelly of human depravity, and visions of untold glory that transport us to the soaring heights of ultimate conquest. The plots and settings are drawn from the living record of the Bible. Series authors and editors were careful to remain faithful to that record. Yet today's sophisticated reading audiences demand background and description. They relate to narrative. In an effort to make the text come alive, each story in this series is presented in a natural framework designed for this audience.

In these stories we see God's people wrestling with their humanity and struggling to find respite for their souls. Each story is unique in its own right. Yet two common threads run through the fabric of their stories and ours. The first is the thread of the bitter curse of sin. The second is the golden thread of salvation in Christ Jesus. We can readily identify with both, for we share these same two themes with all of God's people. Their stories, like ours, rest forever in God's abiding grace.

Kenneth Kremer, Series Editor

THE RELUCTANT PREACHER

With good reason, many people are afraid of fire. It spreads. It kills. It destroys. We respect those who fight fires and rescue people entrapped by them. They risk their own lives to save others. Many firefighters have gone into burning buildings to rescue someone trapped and perishing in the flames. What a relief for a person gasping and choking to see the silhouette of someone who can help! Unfortunately, at times even firefighters themselves become victims in need of rescue.

So it was with God's prophet Jonah. God had sent him to Israel to rescue people from the sin that leads to the fires of hell. The lifeline Jonah extended to them was the Word of God. But Jonah was an extraordinary person with extraordinary talents. God gave to Jonah the rare mission of extending the lifeline of his enduring promises to the gentile people of Nineveh. They too were to be included in God's plan of salvation. Only God could rescue Nineveh. Only God could rescue Israel. And only God could rescue Jonah, the rescuer in need of rescuing.

Jonah's is more than a timeless and fanciful tale. It is reliable truth about God's compassionate and saving heart. It was as true then as it is now: "Salvation comes from the LORD" (Jonah 2:9).

Jonah carefully placed on his bed what he thought he'd need for the journey: a tunic, a cloak to fight off the cold nights, a staff that had stood in the corner for the rough roads, some extra food, and, yes, a new pair of sandals. He'd better not forget his money pouch because there would be a one-way ticket to buy. How far would Jonah actually have to go to get away? He'd also miss the bare confines of his tiny room. The little window framed the olive trees outside as if it were a work of art hanging on the cool stone wall. He'd also miss his small Galilean village. Even though nothing exciting ever happened in Gath Hepher and no one famous ever came from Galilee, he would still miss this place. Jonah had no idea where he was going—except away. Far, far away. He just couldn't do what his Lord was asking him to do. Was it really the Lord who was asking? Was he mistaken? The Lord had always made his message clear before. Why should Jonah doubt it this time? The message didn't seem to make sense.

It wasn't that Jonah was afraid of hard work, rejection, or being a spokesperson for the one true God. He'd done it before. He had the privilege of going to Samaria, the capital of the Northern Kingdom of Israel, where he had an audience with the King of Israel himself, Jeroboam II. The Lord had good news for Jonah: there was going to be a renaissance of sorts in Israel, and King Jeroboam was going to oversee it. What a change that would be from the past! The Israelites had lost territory after territory. They were the laughingstock of neighboring lands. All the nation's wealth went down the drain in tribute to other peoples more powerful than they. These misfortunes were soon going to change. The Lord had revealed it.

Things did get better! Jonah had been privileged to see it. Through conquest and acquisition, Jeroboam had expanded the eastern boundaries of Israel. It now reached limits they hadn't seen since the reigns of Kings David and Solomon during the golden age of the monarchy. Soon tributes from these conquered lands began to flow into Israel's coffers. This cash flow triggered unprecedented wealth and opulence—for those on top at least. What a privilege it was to convey good news for a change! What a joy to see that things turned out exactly as the Lord had said they would!

For once others were treating the Israelites as the people of promise the Lord had said they were. Didn't everyone know that salvation was from the Jews? The Prophet—the promised Messiah-King—was to come from this nation and do his work within it. Wasn't this what the good Lord intended when he approached Abram on that starry night, promising to make him into a great nation and to give him a great land? Through Abram and the nation descended from him, the Lord would bless everyone on earth. The Lord had long ago created this nation from the offspring of an aged and infertile couple. The Lord had nurtured this nation from a clannish group of captive slaves in Egypt. He had led them to the very land he had promised, on oath, to Abraham—a land he had said he would give to the patriarch's descendants.

Before entering the Promised Land under Moses' leadership, the Lord gave these special people his Law at Mount

Sinai. This Law was his pledge to be their God. His people's response was their pledge to be his people. They would show they were his people by living lives of obedience to his commands. God's commands would serve as a protective hedge around his chosen people. In keeping them, they would look and act differently from the other nations that surrounded them. As the Lord's chosen people, they would be different from other nations. They would be his cradle of salvation for the world. Jonah was proud of his heritage as a Hebrew. It was about time they experienced a little prosperity.

Not that the Israelites deserved it. They hadn't always looked and acted so much differently than the infidel nations around them. Jonah had to admit to himself that even in Israel's present outward prosperity, there was much spiritual poverty. The rich cared little for the poor and downtrodden. Why should they care? They had what they needed to fill their homes and their bellies. It seemed the more God blessed them outwardly, the more spiritually famished they became. Their religion had become a sham; they had let it degenerate into a mere shell; they had cut the heart out of it. They had no heart for the Lord and no heart for one another. No longer were they living in repentance. No longer did they walk in faith with the Lord who would bring Christ into the world through them. Jonah had to admit that what seemed to be a new high point in Israel's history was, in reality, a low point. The Israelites were ripe for God's judgment.

Jonah, however, didn't want to be a channel for God's judgment. After all, Jonah's name meant "dove," a messenger of peace and a symbol for God's Spirit. It would have been more fitting if the Lord had given him good news to bolster the king. He wouldn't even have minded if the Lord had given him honest words of condemnation and judgment for Israel. At least it would have been evidence that the Lord still cared for his people. Didn't the Lord want his people to turn back to him? Didn't he want them to wait for the fulfillment of his promise to send a deliverer, One whom he himself would anoint? The Lord's psalmist had prayed, "Do not hand over the life of your dove to wild beasts; do not forget the lives of your afflicted people forever" (Psalm 74:19). What the Lord was asking of Jonah was hard—very hard. In fact, it was unprecedented in Israel's history.

It seemed unbelievable, but the Lord was not calling Jonah to go preach against Israel but Nineveh. The Lord's words still echoed in his cranium: "Go to the great city of Nineveh and preach against it, because its wickedness has come up before me." It was not as if Jonah had ever been there, but he knew Nineveh wasn't some harmless backwoods, bumpkinly town like Gath Hepher. It was a huge metropolis—the political center of Assyria.

Assyria was Israel's archenemy. The Assyrians were a wicked, warlike people—brutal barbarians who loved to see their victims writhe in pain. Chopping off limbs, putting out eyes, pulling out tongues and teeth, impaling on poles, and skinning alive—these were their favorite means of torture for those who refused to submit to them. They loved to pile up the bodies—and the skins—of the insubordinate, to intimidate

Nineveh and the Assyrians

Scripture names Nimrod as Nineveh's founder, along with the cities of Rehoboth Ir, Calah, and Resen. These cities seem to constitute what might be referred to as "Greater Nineveh," the main city and its suburbs.

Nineveh itself was a walled city some 3 miles long and 1.5 miles wide. In some places its walls were 100 feet high with 15 towers, each guarded by a stone lion. The walls were wide enough for three chariots to travel side by side along the top of the bulwark.

In Sennacherib's time (704–682 B.C.) Nineveh boasted temples, fortifications, parks, a botanical garden, and a zoo. He built a royal residence of 71 rooms with walls deco rated with sculpted slabs of stone. The library of Ashurbanipal contained 22,000 volumes of inscribed clay tablets. Nineveh had an elaborate water system that eventually became its undoing. An alliance of the Medes, Babylonians, and Scythians destroyed the city in 612 B.C. by releasing the city's water supply into the Khoser River. The river overflowed its banks, dissolving the sun-dried bricks from which much of Nineveh had been built. Another of God's prophets, Nahum, foretold that Nineveh would meet its end in this way (Nahum 2:6,8).

Nineveh was the capital of the nation of Assyria, located between the Tigris and Euphrates Rivers. On one hand, the Assyrians were highly civilized. They had a written language of pictographs and symbols inscribed on clay tablets. In their religion they believed in the existence of many gods. They worshiped their head god, Ashur, in addition to the spirits they believed inhabited many objects in nature. On the other hand, Assyria was barbaric. The Assyrian army was ruthless, burning cities and their inhabitants. They were excessively cruel to their victims, either beheading them, impaling them on stakes, or chopping off their hands.

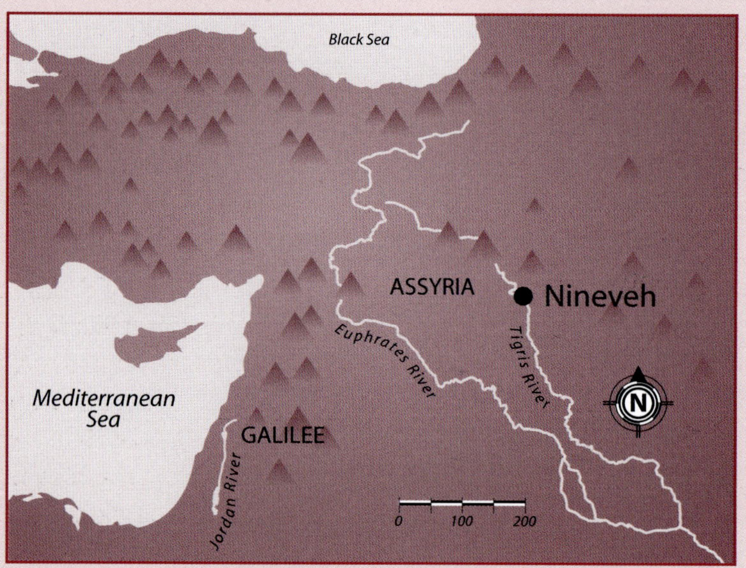

people into bowing to their authority. The mere sight of the Assyrians struck terror into the hearts of nations that had to deal with them. Their religion was disgusting. They were *goyim*—Gentiles. That word stuck in Jonah's throat.

Jonah heard that things hadn't been going so well for Assyria lately. That's good, thought Jonah. Her leaders were preoccupied with conquests on the fringes of the empire. They weren't taking care of the holdings they already had. Assyria was like a servant girl carrying too many water pots and cooking implements into her kitchen. Some fell out of her grasp. Assyria's provinces used the opportunity to rebel against her tyranny. So at the moment, Assyria was relatively weak. Her fate as a nation teetered in the balance between oblivion and opulence. Hopefully—for Israel's sake—it would be the former. It was what heathen people deserved for their detestable sins of greed and idolatry.

Jonah could already see what might happen if he went to Nineveh and preached just what the Lord had told him to preach: "forty more days and Nineveh will be destroyed." The Ninevites could ignore, ridicule, and reject his message. And this was not taking into account what they might do to him. Surely the Lord would keep his word and destroy Nineveh, and Assyria itself would fall apart. That would be a blessing. They'd get what they deserved. Jonah could just imagine what it would be like to bring the good news back to Israel: As a result of his preaching, the Lord had eliminated the greatest of Israel's enemies. He had raised his mighty hand on behalf of his people. They might even regard Jonah as a hero.

But what if Nineveh actually did repent? What if they somehow came to know the God of Israel as the God of forgiveness and mercy? The Lord would spare them in his patience and even bless them as he had Israel. Jonah didn't even want to think about that possibility. The Assyrians could then rise up as an even mightier nation to utterly destroy the people of God. Maybe that was the Lord's plan all along. He would use a prosperous Assyria as a hammer to pound his own people into the ground. If Israel didn't change, if her people refused to quit their pride and hypocrisy, why shouldn't he do this?

There was another dimension Jonah hadn't yet thought of—a personal one. Suppose word got back to Israel that Jonah was the one who had caused a massive turnaround in the hearts of the Ninevites. Would his own people brand him a traitor and reject him as their enemy? Who would listen to him then? He would be like a little boy who fed and befriended a stray wolf pup, only to have that wolf in its maturity destroy his father's flock of sheep!

Jonah doubted that he had heard the Lord correctly. Did God really say that he was to go to Nineveh? Maybe that's not what God meant. Maybe there was some other way. Jonah didn't want to think about it too long. Instead, he would just run the other way. Maybe then he could clear his mind and think about the possibilities of the Lord's call another day. Jonah reasoned that he wasn't really saying "No"; he was just saying, "Not now." It's not as though he could get away from God. He knew what David had written. He knew the words well: "Where can I go from your Spirit? Where can I flee from your presence? If I go up to the heavens, you are there; if I make my bed in the depths, you are there. If I rise on the wings of the dawn, if I settle on the far side of the sea, even there your hand will guide me, your right hand will hold me fast" (Psalm 139:7-10).

Jonah would test those words. To the far side of the sea he would go. But in going, why did he feel so much like Adam hiding from the searching eyes of God? Why did he feel as David must have felt after committing adultery with Bathsheba? It was as though he was dying from the inside out. But the Lord was asking something of him he just didn't have within himself to do. He tried not to think about it. Like a giant magnet, the port city of Joppa on the Mediterranean Sea pulled him. He had to focus on that now. He tried to ignore the ice cube of pain that formed inside his soul, the shivers of fear branching out to each extremity.

The way to Joppa, the nearest seaport, was rugged with few opportunities for stopping along the way. Perhaps he could stay at some small town one night and sleep under the stars another. By the third day, his 60-mile journey should be complete. Then he would seek out a ship—maybe a passenger ship, maybe a cargo ship—and see how far away he could go. Still there was a strong tug to unpack his bag and give in to the Lord's call. No, he couldn't. "Focus on the port," he told himself. "Once you're on a ship, there will be no turning back." So he closed up the garment bag and left the little room in his house, slamming the door behind him.

In Joppa, Jonah descended the ramparts to the docks. Gravity seemed to pull him down to the shipyard. He could smell the salty freshness of the water below. It would be easy to find room on one of the many ships loading their crates of cargo.

There was one, a Phoenician cargo ship that appeared to be accepting passengers. It looked like a big wooden duck floating gracefully along the shore. It was docked with its sails rolled up against the masts, ready to be unfurled at any moment, like flags. Both forward oars stuck proudly out of the water like soldiers guarding their silver treasures on board. Was that the captain standing there? Jonah asked if there was still room.

"How far do you want to go?" the captain asked.

"What's your final port before turning around?" Jonah inquired.

"Tartessus," the captain replied. "Some people call it Tarshish. It's about 2,000 miles away from here." Tartessus was an ancient Phoenician colony on the southwestern coast of Spain, on the end of the Mediterranean Sea, opposite Israel. Phoenician sailors called it the *end of the line*.

"Here's my fare," announced Jonah. "The farther away, the better."

Chills went through Jonah's body as he boarded the ship. He glanced up at the sails. Hardly one of them moved. The sea was as calm as he had ever seen it, almost as smooth as a rippled pane of glass. The chill must have come from the coolness inside his soul, not the gentle Mediterranean breezes.

Maybe he should turn around, walk the gangplank back to shore, and go back home. No. He'd come this far. Going back would mean that he would have to deal with the Lord's instructions for him to go to Nineveh. He just couldn't.

Before long the cargo was all on board and safely stored on and below deck. Finally, the remainder of the passengers—mostly crewmen—boarded the ship. Then the small vessel left its safe harbor. Soon, only sea and blue sky separated Jonah from land. Although the ship would roughly follow the shoreline on its journey, the people on land began to look like scurrying ants on their sandy hills as they faded into the distance. Now there really was no turning back!

It was not difficult to blend with the men of the crew, nor was it difficult to understand their Canaanite dialect. It wasn't much different from his native Hebrew. There was someone from nearly every Phoenician colony. Great cities like Utica, Tyre, Sidon, and Tartessus, as well as port cities on Rhodes, Crete, and Cyprus were represented in this eager mix of men. "I can't wait to get home to Cyprus," said one. "I'll have a short leave to be with my family, then off to sea again. Where are you going?" he asked Jonah. The sailor caught him off guard with this direct question. The ears of the other sailors perked up as they leaned in to hear his reply.

"You might say I'm just getting away for a while," Jonah admitted reluctantly. What business was it of theirs anyway? They were *goyim,* probably uninterested in, and certainly unworthy of knowing, Jonah's God or his mission. Maybe a vague reply would get them off of his trail. "My God has very high expectations of where I should be going and what I should be doing," he explained. "I just need to get away for a while."

The sailors let his vague reply stand without further interrogation. They had work to do. As they were about to scatter to their respective tasks, Jonah saw an opportunity to rest. He was exhausted. "I'm dead tired from the journey here," he said. "Is there someplace I can go to sleep for a while?"

"It's quiet down in the cargo hold," one said. "Go below deck to the forward compartment. There are some piles of cloth and rolls of textiles. You might be comfortable there."

Jonah found a ladder sticking up through an open hatch leading to the compartments below deck. It was dark and dank down there. A few hatches and tiny openings pierced the darkness, bringing light and air from above. The smell of the pitch coating the bent boards of the ship mixed with the sweet smell of spices and perfumes being transported to ports beyond. He found a soft spot among some linen swatches and bunched up some cotton fabric for a makeshift pillow. With his bag of possessions securely at his side, he removed his sandals and lay down.

As he reflected on the events of the past few days—the Lord's call and Jonah's hasty reaction—his thoughts ran together. Like a giant storm within, his conscience accused him in waves of guilt. He was running from the Lord. But the Lord wanted him to save infidels! Why waste his precious words when his own people so desperately needed them? But God had spoken. Jonah just didn't listen. It didn't feel right to go where God wanted, yet it was wrong to run away. His spirit sank. What could he do, jump overboard and swim back to shore? Ask the captain to turn the boat around? Jonah had made his bed; now he had to lie in it. He resolved not to think about it any longer. He would do nothing. Like a floating cradle, the rocking motion of the ship soothed him. But was the ship swaying and bobbing more than usual? Was that the pounding of waves he was hearing? He didn't care. He just wanted to sleep. Soon the dark clouds in his mind stilled the winds of emotion that had swept through his chilly soul. Darkness had overtaken him. He fell into a deep, deep sleep.

On deck it was anything but calm. The clear sky had given way to clouds. A wall of wind came out of nowhere and stirred the sea into a fury. Waves tossed around the tiny ship like a cat playing with a mouse soon to become its prey. As if in pain, the ship groaned under the stress of the shifting sea. The maritime forces nearly pulled it apart like a basket being stretched by quarreling children. Anything left on deck slid back and forth from stem to stern and from port to starboard. The sailors themselves were no exception. They scurried to tie down tools and supplies; they climbed the masts, risking life and limb to loosen the rigging and lower the sails. They clung for dear life to the masts and the rails—and to one another. Waves of fear swept over them. There wasn't a thing they could do.

Except pray. There certainly was no shortage of gods to pray to; nearly every man had his own. Perhaps Baal, the chief god responsible for the forces of nature, could do something. There was always his feminine counterpart, Ashtoreth, the nature goddess whom they dubbed the "Queen of Heaven." They could call on one of the sons of Siddik, overseers of ships and navigation, or Melgart, the god of the sea. Tanith was also a goddess of the elements and would be a likely choice. So they prayed. But the storm prevailed.

In a final effort to stabilize the breaking ship, they began to toss cargo overboard. The shifting sea irreverently swallowed precious glass, pottery, metals, and fine linen. The lighter load, however, had little effect on the flailing vessel.

The captain noticed that someone had been missing in all of this commotion. Where was that fellow who was escaping from his misty past? Was he still below deck as the sailors had indicated when they were down there moving cargo? How could he sleep through all of this? Why wasn't he calling on his god? The captain went to find out.

Down he went into the cargo hold, spotting Jonah right away. He shook Jonah's slumbering body, as if the sea hadn't done a good enough job of it. "How can you be sleeping?" he asked. "Get up and call on your god! Maybe he'll notice us and do something so that we don't perish in this storm."

Rubbing his eyes and shaking the sluggishness from his mind, Jonah began to perceive what the commotion around him was all about. He reflected on the captain's words. He could feel the blood rush up his neck and flush his face. Jonah was angry. Who was this man—a mere infidel—to tell him when and where to pray to his God? What did he know about Yahweh, the Lord—the one true God who made all things and rules all things? He was also embarrassed. If there was trouble, why hadn't Jonah noticed it first? Why hadn't he been the one to suggest praying to the Lord for deliverance? It was proof that he definitely was not the Lord's man for Nineveh. Jonah fought the rollicking ship, the pounding waves, and the gale force winds and made his way to the main deck.

If he didn't know better, he would have thought the sailors were playing some kind of game of chance. With small pieces of driftwood in a broken packing crate, they were casting lots. It didn't take long before Jonah discovered they were actually drawing lots to see which person on board was responsible for the storm that was pummeling them. It was no secret that he was the offending stick in the crate. "Tell us, who is responsible for making all this trouble for us? What do you do? Where do you come from? What is your country? From what people are you?" Like blasts of wind, their questions battered him.

"I am a Hebrew, and I worship the LORD, the God of heaven, who made the sea and the land," he replied. He told them of his God whose hands held the land and the sea, the sky and the stars. He related how this God had chosen a nation to bless all other nations. He showed how throughout Israel's history, this God had punished wickedness, rebellion, and sin, but had also continually forgiven those who acknowledged their sin and looked to God's promised Anointed One as their deliverer.

The sailors began to put two and two together. Earlier Jonah had admitted to running away from the expectations of his God. If this God really was the Lord of lords and held the sky and the sea at bay, this storm could be a display of this God's displeasure with Jonah. That would make them coconspirators in Jonah's little plan! A new fear began to overwhelm them. The severe storm was nothing by comparison. Would they have to engage in combat with this almighty God who punishes sin and forgives sinners? "What have you done?" they asked Jonah in desperation.

Yes, what had he done? That was a good question. Almost in reply, the sea answered with even more fury. "What should we do to you to make the sea calm down for us?" they asked.

"Pick me up and throw me into the sea," Jonah suggested. He wasn't kidding. "The sea will become calm if you do. I know it's my fault that this storm has come upon you." Jonah reasoned that it would be better if one guilty person perished rather than many. And he knew he was the guilty one. How could he continue to put these sailors through such a tormenting ordeal? At least if they threw him overboard, they would be placing him into the hands of his God. That was where Jonah wanted to be. It was too cold, too lonely, and too painful apart from God, as Jonah now was in his great disobedience. He was tired of running from the very one who was reaching out to him.

Jonah's idea didn't sit very well with the sailors, however. That's all they needed: get this Lord of heaven and earth upset by taking the life of his prophet just to save their own skins. Even they knew that life was too precious for that. "We've got to get this guy back to land so he can go where he's supposed to go," they reasoned. They tried to row back, but their attempts were futile. As if to outdo itself, the sea kicked up in the greatest tempest yet. Again they prayed. This time, however, they prayed to Jonah's God. If he was the Lord of heaven and earth, he would hear, and he would help. Furthermore, if he was the Lord who forgave wickedness, rebellion, and sin, perhaps he would forgive them too. They prayed: "O LORD, please do not let us die for taking this man's life. Do not hold us accountable for killing an innocent man, for you, O LORD, have done as you pleased." With two crewmen holding Jonah by the arms and two by the legs, they threw him overboard. They returned Jonah to the hands of his God, and now—of their God too!

To the sailors' utter amazement, the sea immediately became calm. Jonah had been the problem. And his God had been the solution! They spoke to one another in wonder at the secret they had discovered. They didn't know what they revered more, this Lord's power or his compassion. It was amazing to them that he would take time to hear and answer their prayers. The seamen gathered up personal treasures and offered them to the Lord. They pledged their loyalty and devotion to the God of the Hebrews—Jonah's God.

Jonah hit the water with a slap. It stung his side and chest as if he had run into a wall. The voices of the sailors and the sight of the ship faded quickly as the sensation of the cold water surrounded him. Salt burned his eyes, nostrils, and lips. Instinctively he tried swimming for what seemed to be hours, but what progress he made, he couldn't even tell. Before long a dull but intense pain paralyzed him and made it impossible for him to stay afloat. He felt himself going down. He struggled to the surface. One more gasp of breath and one more look at the breaking clouds. Would he ever breathe air or see the sun again? He felt himself going down again. He didn't know which was worse: the pain or the cold. Maybe they were one and the same.

This time he couldn't fight his way to the surface. The more he clawed his way up, the farther down he sank. It hurt to open his eyes in the salty soup. He stopped trying. He felt the swirling motion of the water and the undercurrents pulling him deeper and deeper into his watery grave. The weight of the water pressing around him was enormous. The deeper he went, the colder it got. But it didn't matter much. Feeling had nearly left his body. Strands of seaweed wound around his head, neck, arms, and legs like the tentacles of an octopus. The more he struggled to free himself, the more entangled he became. A quick glance through the murky water revealed rocky crags and ledges towering over him. Consciousness faded in and out. He felt life and warmth flow from his body. Soon it would all be over.

THE LORD SENT A FISH

Was he thinking or was he praying? Thoughts to himself and thoughts to his God blended together in one stream of awareness. Was he now paying for his own transgressions? Would he be cut off from life, doomed to be separated from God forever in the flames of sheol? This was the true destination of his flight from God, wasn't it? It wasn't Tartessus at all! Only one gasp—a mere heartbeat—separated him from such a fate. He dared to come before the Lord in spirit: "LORD, I've alienated myself from you. I deserve to be cut off from you forever. But in the name of Israel's Hope, have mercy on me and help me. I seek your presence and your love. Whether I live or die, I am yours."

In his mind's eye, he could see the Lord's temple in Jerusalem. God's holy presence was there with his people. He could see the priests offering the lives of innocent animal victims for their guilty human counterparts. This ongoing bloodbath foreshadowed what the Messiah would do. Jonah believed that. No animal blood could erase sin, but his Lord's blood could. God was merciful—he knew that. David had said it after his lapse: "Against you, you only, have I sinned and done what is evil in your sight, so that you are proved right when you speak and justified when you judge. Hide your face from my sins and blot out all my iniquity. Create in me a pure heart, O God, and renew a steadfast spirit within me. Do not cast me from your presence or take your Holy Spirit from me" (Psalm 51:4,9-11).

Jonah now felt a slight new sensation—warmth. At first he couldn't tell if it came from inside his being or outside.

A Great Fish

The great fish is the one aspect of the Jonah account that is most difficult for critics to swallow. The King James Version confuses the issue in the way it translates Jesus' words in Matthew 12:40: "For as Jonas was three days and three nights in the whale's belly . . ." In the Greek language there is no such word as *whale.* As is indicated in the Hebrew text of the book of Jonah, it was a large sea creature or a huge fish of some kind. A whale's throat would have been too narrow to swallow a human being. Besides, whales are rare in the Mediterranean Sea.

There have been many conjectures as to what kind of fish this was. Best guesses seem to support a large type of shark or sea dog, a creature common in the Mediterranean, particularly in deep water. Some shark species can get to be 25 feet long and weigh in at between 300 and 1,500 pounds. They have as many as four hundred sharp teeth arranged in six rows, with throats large enough to easily swallow a human being. One such shark swallowed whole an entire horse!

In 1758 a sailor on the Mediterranean Sea fell overboard in stormy weather only to be swallowed by one of these sharks. His captain ordered that the ship's gun be fired at the shark. The cannon ball hit its target, causing the fish to vomit up the swallowed sailor alive and unharmed. (*Commentary on the Old Testament: New Updated Edition*, Keil & Delitzsch, Hendrickson Publishers, Inc., 1996.)

What is significant in the Jonah account is that the Lord himself provided the fish at the right place and the right time to swallow Jonah. In this fish the Lord kept Jonah alive for three days and then caused it to spit Jonah out unharmed onto land. This was no fluke of nature. It was a miracle of Jonah's almighty and compassionate God.

This slimy embrace was quite a contrast from the icy tomb he had been in just a moment before! But where was he now? Everything was dark, even when he dared to open his eyes. He heard squishing sounds interspersed with gurgles and growls. A rhythmic thumping punctuated everything he heard. Was it a heartbeat? A putrid stench invaded his nostrils. It was almost like a combination of rotting flesh and vomitous bile. He wondered: Had he been swallowed alive? Some monster of the deep must have happened by and consumed him whole! "Happened by," had he thought? No, this was not a coincidence. This was the Lord. He had sent this rescue, hadn't he? Jonah's life wasn't over.

His thoughts again merged into prayer. Verses and verses of psalms came to him. In youth he had learned them well. Their melodies resounded in his memory and made them easy to recall. He again made them his own. He recalled how he had called out to God from the depths of the ocean: "In my distress I called to the LORD, and he answered me. From the depths of the grave I called for help, and you listened to my cry. You hurled me into the deep, into the very heart of the seas, and the currents swirled about me; all your waves and breakers swept over me. I said, 'I have been banished from your sight; yet I will look again toward your holy temple.' The engulfing waters threatened me, the deep surrounded me; seaweed was wrapped around my head. To the roots of the mountains I sank down; the earth beneath barred me in forever."

God hadn't left him in that helpless state, however. He had provided this fish to rescue him and carry him to land.

THE LORD SENT A FISH

Jonah continued praying: "But you brought my life up from the pit, O LORD my God. When my life was ebbing away, I remembered you, LORD, and my prayer rose to you, to your holy temple. Those who cling to worthless idols forfeit the grace that could be theirs. But I, with a song of thanksgiving, will sacrifice to you. What I have vowed I will make good. Salvation comes from the LORD."

His thoughts halted as his consciousness waned. Just as he had experienced earlier when he was nearly drowning in the depths of the sea, Jonah once again lost all track of time. The darkness inside the sea creature made it impossible for him to tell if it was day or night. It was hard to sleep, but it was also hard to stay awake. He felt his thoughts dissolving in the fluid of his mind. He wouldn't fight it any longer—he couldn't. Whatever his Lord wanted was fine with him. What mattered was that he was safe. He, like the sea creature, was in the hands of the almighty Lord of heaven and earth. There was no better place to be regardless of earthly location.

Jonah was unsure about how long he had been inside the huge fish. But suddenly he found himself on dry land. The side of his body on which he landed on hard ground throbbed with a dull ache. He awoke in a sea of sunlight, dry and warm. A Mediterranean breeze massaged his newfound consciousness until he was fully awake. The green of the tamarisk and sycamore fig trees shimmered in a light breeze. The shoreline seemed more verdant than it ever had before. The air was fresher than he could ever remember. Even the songs of the birds and calls of the gulls that swooped overhead were more musical than what he recalled. It was as if his bout with the sea had erased years of grime and dullness from his perception of life. He felt like a new person.

Later Jonah concluded that he had been in the belly of this sea creature the better part of three days. The great beast that had swallowed him had vomited him up onto land.

Joppa wasn't far up the coastline. He ended up not far from where he had started. It made Jonah chuckle. This brute monster had been more obedient to the Lord's command than he had! The fish better suited the Lord's purposes than Jonah did!

That was going to change. If the Lord wanted him to go somewhere off the beaten path to speak the praises of the God of Israel, he would go. This God had delivered him from death, and not just death in a watery grave. God had delivered him from the prospect of eternally dying into an existence of separation from the Lord's life and love. If God could do this for a rebellious prophet who should know better, God could also do this for a heathen people who had no knowledge of anything better. The Lord was compassionate—Jonah knew that. That he was here—living, breathing, and believing—was proof of the Lord's compassion. Jonah knew he was a walking miracle—a testimony to the power and love of the one true God.

Jonah also knew his Lord had forgiven him. But would he ever again consider Jonah worthy of doing his work? He could understand if he wouldn't. Why should he? Would Jonah run away again? Maybe he could go back to Gath Hepher and his little room and find menial work there in town. Perhaps there was a sheepherder who needed a hand. Maybe he could stay in Joppa and help load cargo onto ships. This bothered him though. His training was as a prophet; it was how Jonah made his living. He couldn't picture himself doing anything else. The matter was the Lord's to decide. One thing was for certain: Jonah was the Lord's, and did he have a story to tell about how the Lord gave him a new beginning and a renewed purpose for living. Salvation was the Lord's! Just the thought of what he had been through made his heart race, his body shiver, and his head sweat. Would he ever be the same again? Hopefully not!

Jonah found his way up the coastline on the road to Joppa. Soon he saw the city perched on its rocky seaside ledge. The usual flurry of activity around the docks continued; it was Joppa's livelihood. He headed toward the movement of people. Maybe he could find some water and food. Someone might be willing to listen to his story of how his compassionate God had rescued him and had given him a new lease on life. Jonah would return. Not just to Israel and his home in Gath Hepher. He would return to his Lord. This time he would trust implicitly the God of his redemption. Only in the Lord was he truly alive.

IN COMPASSION, THE LORD SENT A REPRIEVE

Jonah awoke well rested. The sunlight streaming in through his bedroom window bathed him in warmth. The events of the past few days seemed like a hazy mist evaporating in the sun's rays. But he hadn't forgotten. How could he ever forget being in that watery grave for three days and then coming to life again? How could he ignore standing at the edge of a cliff, staring into the gaping jaws of hell and having none other than God personally pull him back to life? It all seemed like a dream, but he hadn't forgotten.

God hadn't forgotten Jonah either. His word came to Jonah a second time, in spite of all that had happened. It was like a stroke out of the blue, just as it had been the first time. The Lord said, "Go to the great city of Nineveh and proclaim to it the message I give you." There were no threats. There was no dredging up Jonah's flight as a reminder of his unworthiness or a warning against doing it again. There was only a command. A call. A great commission. They would do this together, Jonah and his Lord God. God was giving him a second chance. He would have the opportunity to right what he had formerly done wrong. The Lord really had forgiven him. He hadn't written Jonah off as a worthless deserter.

Jonah thought of his ancestors in the Garden of Eden. Adam and Eve had hid in fear from their almighty Creator-God only to have him announce the greatest promise ever made. God would give humanity a second chance through the woman's offspring. He would one day send his own offspring to live and die on behalf of his rebellious creatures. Jonah also thought of Jacob staring upward at the steps of a ladder that stretched all the way to heaven. Angels were moving up and down its stairs as they served him. It was God's assurance that he hadn't turned his back on Jacob, in spite of Jacob's deceitfulness and trickery. Jonah's thoughts wandered to David, an adulterer and murderer. Although David had lost a child conceived in sin, he hadn't lost the Lord who brought him to see his sin and repent. Now the Lord showed Jonah that same compassion. Jonah was elated at the thought.

This time he wouldn't hesitate. He would pack quickly, determine the fastest route to Nineveh, and go. He threw some belongings together, wrapped them in an extra cloak, and off he went. This time he headed out of Gath Hepher in the opposite direction from the way he had gone before. The 600-mile journey northeast would be long and oppressive. It would take over a month, depending on where he would stay overnight along the way and whether or not he would travel on the Sabbath. Yet when compared with his previous flight, this journey would seem brief and pleasant. This time he was going with God, not against him. Before long he would be there.

When he arrived, Jonah could see the vast city in the distance. It truly was a great spectacle—a wonder, not only in size but also in influence. The city proper sprawled out and absorbed its neighbors, forming a bustling hub of vigorous activity in every direction, as far as Jonah's eyes could see. Like a dried and cracked mud puddle, Nineveh's sunbaked brick buildings, placid aqueducts, and dusty streets lay in front of him. Through the city flowed the Khoser River. On the other end of the city, outside the city walls, it joined with the Tigris.

Jonah could pick out landmarks: an impressive palace, a temple to some Assyrian god with its ziggurat towers, a library, a marketplace, and a splash of green that was a park. Tree-lined boulevards made their way through the city and were bordered with houses and shops, nearly each one with its own central courtyard. Gardens and orchards of figs, olives, pomegranates, almonds, mulberries, and other tropical fruit trees surrounded many of the houses. Around the outskirts of the city, groves of trees grew and grain fields ripened, food for the city's inhabitants and their animals.

The city's features grew larger and more distinct as Jonah came nearer. He approached the city gate and looked at the two impressive guard towers looming high above him. A sculpture of a winged bull flanked each, poised as if to swoop down and gore any enemy who dared to attack the great city. What a greeting, especially for someone who was coming as an outsider to bring a message of doom and gloom! How would these strange, brutal people receive him? He was still convinced these infidels would refuse to listen to God. They would probably ignore him or laugh him off as some kind of raving lunatic. Maybe they would question him and expel him as a foreigner right here at the city gate. Then he could at least say that he tried.

But it didn't work that way. Jonah made his way into the city and started down the main street toward a marketplace.

All along the way, beggars, with their filthy, unkempt hands, reached out, pleading for whatever a passerby might offer them. There were people everywhere. With so many people, where would he begin? It would take at least three days just to travel from one end of the city to the other, up and down its major streets, penetrating its boroughs of houses. Jonah headed straight for the marketplace to focus on the people there. Considering the commerce and trade that went on there, maybe here people would tend to be more open to what a foreigner would have to say.

Jonah found people. They were busy with the chores of life, of buying and selling, of surviving. Without hesitation he began to preach. At first only a few stopped; most kept going. Once a small crowd had gathered, more people joined them. They were more curious as to why the others were standing there than they were about Jonah's message. "Listen to me," Jonah announced. "I have some important news. The LORD—the one true God—has revealed something amazing about Nineveh's future. In 40 days Nineveh will be destroyed! The LORD will no longer tolerate your evil ways, your lack of compassion for the poor and needy, the immorality and depravity of your worship, and the untold horrors you have inflicted on others. He's giving you 40 days to turn to him as your LORD. He is compassionate and forgiving. He promised mankind a deliverer who would come from the Hebrew people. This great hero from God will destroy evil and death forever. For the sake of this promise, God will not bring this disaster on you. Trust him and turn away from your sins. Look in faith to his love and his promise."

At first, the people stared at Jonah in disbelief, amazed that he would go around saying something that seemed so foolish. This was mighty Nineveh, the city of kings and nobles, Assyria's badge of honor. She had fended off the most brutal of attackers and maintained her victory and her valor. Nineveh destroyed? But their skepticism turned to curiosity. "Who are you? How do you know this God of yours is going to do such a terrible thing? Why should we believe you?"

Jonah answered: "I am living proof of the Lord's justice and mercy. He told me to come here, and at first, I fled by sea in the opposite direction. Then he sent a storm that nearly capsized the ship. The LORD made it clear that it was because of me that this was happening. I had done a terrible thing. The only answer was to have the sailors throw me overboard in an effort to quell the fury of the storm and God's wrath. They threw me overboard, and immediately the storm stopped.

"As I sank to the ocean's bottom, I nearly drowned. All I could do was lean on the LORD's mercy. In the throes of the deep, I called out to him for help. And you'll be amazed—he answered me! He rescued me by sending a great fish to swallow me, and he kept me alive inside the fish for three days until the fish spit me out onto land! Now he has given me another chance to come to you—living proof that if you turn aside from your evil ways and trust in his mercy, he will have compassion on you too. I am your sign from God that his word is true!"

At this, whispers spread through the growing crowd

like the sound of crickets in an evening field. "That Hebrew was spared from destruction by his God who sent a big fish to rescue him. Now he says his God is going to destroy us in 40 days if we don't turn from our evil ways and trust him." Jonah hardly needed to continue. "Forty more days and Nineveh will be destroyed" was the message that soon went from one end of the city to the other. Most of those who heard it didn't bother about the messenger. They were too occupied with the message. It came from the Lord of heaven and earth. Even storms obeyed his bidding. Why shouldn't they obey? The Ninevites believed. They believed Jonah's message. They believed in Jonah's angry, righteous God. But they believed in his enduring compassion and his promise of redemption.

As often happens in times of human tragedy, the message seemed to bring the population of Nineveh together. Leaders began to emerge from the gathering crowds; they organized the masses of people. Together they agreed that their conduct had not been very noble or exemplary. They had angered the God who created them. Therefore, they decided that a fast should be declared. This would show their remorse for the depraved lives they had lived. Everyone from the youngest to the oldest and from the peasants to the king's nobles should wear sackcloth—a sign of mourning and grief in the ancient world.

The people wondered how their king would take the news. Would he put down the commotion and make an example of those who led it? Or would he join in, giving his support for an action that seemed so urgent and necessary?

The people didn't have to wait long for their answer. Somehow the king had already learned the news. As he sat in his official garb on his throne in his elaborate palace, he was surrounded by scenes of his triumphs carved into the walls. It was as if both his life and the collective existence of Nineveh paraded before his eyes and the eyes of an all-seeing, all-knowing, almighty God. Was the deportation of entire populations, the torture of victims, and the separation of families something to be proud of? Could any Assyrian gods truly quell the sea or influence its creatures? Their civilization and community deserved to be wiped from the face of the earth and blotted out from history. Would God relent?

The king arose from his throne. He removed his official kingly garb, beautifully woven in its color and intricacy, and unceremoniously threw it to the ground. In its place he donned the sackcloth he had requested his attendants to bring. He exited his palace, went out to a city street, and sat down in the dust and dirt. That is what he and these people were before God—dirt. They were dust, and they would become dust at the behest of God.

In this unlikely position, the king summoned his nobles and his attendants. "Write down the following and have it read in every corner of Nineveh and its suburbs: BY THE DECREE OF THE KING AND HIS NOBLES: DO NOT LET ANY MAN OR BEAST, HERD OR FLOCK, TASTE ANYTHING; DO NOT LET THEM EAT OR DRINK. BUT LET MAN AND BEAST BE COVERED WITH SACKCLOTH. LET EVERYONE CALL URGENTLY ON GOD. LET THEM GIVE UP THEIR EVIL WAYS AND THEIR VIOLENCE. WHO KNOWS? GOD MAY YET

RELENT AND WITH COMPASSION TURN FROM HIS FIERCE ANGER SO THAT WE WILL NOT PERISH."

So it was written; so it was done. Even the animals wore the sackcloth their owners wore, as an extension of their grief. For 40 days the people fasted, and life in the great city of Nineveh stood still. The people were sincere in their repentance. There would be no more idolatry, no more immorality, no more brutality—only devotion to this new God and his peace. Surely God would forgive them and grant them a new life as he had for his prophet Jonah. If he was truly a God who forgave wickedness, rebellion, and sin, he would forgive them too.

He did forgive them. The 40 days passed and nothing happened. A scoffer could have said that this was because Jonah's message was all hype in the first place. But no one made that claim. The population of Nineveh knew that God had had compassion on them. That is why he did not bring on them the destruction he had threatened. God credited their faith in his compassion as their righteousness before him. God saw the Ninevites in a new light—not as alabaster carvings in stone. He saw them in the light of his own Son, the Hebrew descendant whose good and holy accomplishments would forever cover their violence and evil. The Son would become a victim, destined to die in their stead under God's all-consuming wrath.

After 40 days the city turned from fast to feast. There was rejoicing from one end of the city to the other. There was rejoicing in heaven too.

Jonah wasn't rejoicing; he was disappointed. He was amazed that his words—no, the Lord's words—were so well received. Nevertheless, he was sure that even though the Ninevites seemed to repent and turn to the Lord, the Lord would still follow through with the judgment he had threatened.

Jonah's old feelings returned. His disappointment quickly turned to rage. It began deep inside, and like a snake's venom, crept through every organ and extremity in Jonah's body. He was angry at the Ninevites and angry with God. What God had allowed went against every grain in his body. He couldn't get over the fact that the Ninevites were heathen. They were the enemy! They were despicable. They hadn't even known who the true God was until Jonah came drifting into town bellowing threats and promises. They didn't deserve God's compassion. They weren't Israelites—God's chosen. Furthermore, a healthy Nineveh and a thriving Assyria could spell the doom of Israel. They could easily rise up and destroy God's people as they had often threatened in the past. These brutes simply said they were sorry for their sin and made a big repentant show, and the Lord backed off of his threat! Couldn't God see beyond this sham? Didn't he know about all of the atrocities in their past? Yet he forgave them! Never mind centuries of wickedness. Never mind the covenant he made with Israel alone.

Jonah knew he shouldn't feel the way he did. But he couldn't help himself. He felt the way he felt. What could he do? If only he could shrink away and disappear. Earlier it had always helped to talk things over with the Lord. Would the Lord even listen to him in this state? He would pray anyway: "O LORD, is this not what I said when I was still at home? That is why I was so quick to flee to Tarshish. I knew that you are a gracious and compassionate God, slow to anger and abounding in love, a God who relents from sending calamity. Now, O LORD, take away my life, for it is better for me to die than to live." There. Right or wrong, he had gotten it off of his chest.

Then came God's answer: "Jonah, do you have any right to be angry?" That was a good question. Jonah thought he did. Maybe he didn't. God was God. If he had dealt with Jonah only in justice and without compassion, Jonah wouldn't even have been there to go to Nineveh. But he was God's own prophet—an Israelite. These people were *goyim*. They should have been nothing in God's sight.

Jonah went farther away to observe from a vantage point east of the city. There was still time for God to carry out his judgment. After all, if he was going to destroy Nineveh—as Jonah was sure he would—Jonah didn't want to be anywhere near the city. The place where he was sitting was hot. There wasn't much vegetation—only dry, sterile earth. A scorching wind blew dust in his face. It stung every exposed pore on his body. The sun beat down on his head, turning his features red and sore. He needed some kind of protection. Perhaps he could build a shelter. Gathering what branches and stubble he could find on the barren terrain, he formed a makeshift tent. From here he could wait and see what was going to happen to

Nineveh. But nothing happened. Nothing.

Jonah's shelter didn't help much. The oppressive sun and wind found their way through the gaps and openings in its flimsy construction. But an amazing thing happened. Right next to his little lean-to, a plant began to grow. It seemed to spring up and get big overnight. The leaves were huge. Was it a castor bean plant or some kind of gourd? It vined up and over his enclosure. What kind of unusual plant this was didn't matter. What mattered was that the Lord had provided it to give him shade! The top of his head, once boiling and burning in the sun, began to feel cool once again. The temperature inside his hut fell several degrees. Jonah was happy. In fact, he was ecstatic. He could watch for the fireworks in air-conditioned comfort. How kind of the Lord to provide such relief!

Night brought further respite from the heat of the day. It was almost too cool. Unfortunately, the relief was short-lived. As dawn arrived, so did disappointment. Jonah's plant didn't look right. It was wilted and droopy. God had sent a worm to chew its way into the plant and suck the life juices right out of it. The plant hung limp and useless. What a waste! It had been so full and verdant. Each leaf had served its purpose like flaps in a tent. Perhaps it would have grown even bigger to bear flowers and fruit. It could have been a tremendous help to Jonah for many days to come. Now it was dead.

To add insult to injury, God had also sent a scorching east wind—the dreaded desert sirocco—that raised the temperature (and Jonah's anger) to an unbearable level. The sun beat down on Jonah's head once again with unrelenting torridity. At first Jonah just felt weak and woozy. Soon his legs turned to rubber. He had to lie down to keep from fainting. How long would he have to suffer like this? "It would be better for me to die than to live like this," he said. And it was all God's fault. What good purpose could this misery serve? How ironic that the God who had almost destroyed him with water now seemed to be doing the same with the sun's fire.

An answer to Jonah's questions came more quickly than he had expected. "Do you have a right to be angry about the vine?" God asked.

Jonah was honest. "I do," he replied. "I am angry enough to die." And he was. Why would the Lord raise up such a beautiful plant to give such comfort only to take it away in a whim? It hadn't even reached its full potential for shade and food. Now, as a result, Jonah was roasting in the blistering desert sun. It seemed as though God was playing with him. He had seen fathers play with their children this way. They would give a child a toy, hide it, and then study their child's puzzled or angry reaction. Angry? Yes, Jonah was angry enough to die. He wished he would.

But the Lord had more to say: "You have been concerned about this vine, though you did not tend it or make it grow. It sprang up overnight and died overnight. But Nineveh has more than a hundred and twenty thousand people who cannot tell their right hand from their left and many cattle as well. Should I not be concerned about that great city?"

It took awhile for things to sink in. Jonah realized the Lord was actually teaching him a lesson with the vine. It had been God's creation, to bless Jonah. It was God's prerogative to cause it to grow and prosper or to bring about its demise. In the same way, God had brought Nineveh and the Assyrians onto the world scene for a purpose. He could use them to bless Israel or to chastise Israel. That too was the Lord's prerogative. Nevertheless, the Ninevites were real people with immortal souls who would perish eternally without the Lord's compassion. Just as that plant was important to Jonah—worthy of being saved—so Nineveh was important to God. In fact, the people of Nineveh were more worthy of being saved than Jonah's plant.

Jonah should have been happy when the Ninevites believed God and repented. He should have rejoiced that God cared enough for them to call them from their wickedness, rebellion, and sin. Only then could they know their need for the descendant from the Hebrews who would save them. They hadn't known up from down as far as worshiping the Lord was concerned. Now they did. Shouldn't that have brought Jonah the same joy as it had brought to God?

Jonah couldn't get the Lord's question out of his mind: "Should I not be concerned about that great city?" The answer seemed so obvious, yet Jonah didn't answer that question. His silence was loud; he knew the answer. Once again he had been foolish. His pride and his prejudice had eaten away at his heart as surely as the worm had sucked the life-juices out of his treasured plant. His self-righteousness left him cold and calloused in the desert heat. Why was he at this vantage point waiting for God to torch Nineveh? He had come 600 miles to carry out his Lord's command. But in his soul, he had never moved one inch from his Israelite home and his elitist Hebrew mindset. Why had the Lord allowed him to live? Why had he allowed the Ninevites to live? It was grace. It was compassion. Jonah's shame gave way to peace. Jonah, *the dove*, would fly again.

First, back to Gath Hepher. Jonah would write down his experiences—not just the good things but things that were not so flattering too. The fact that God used him as his prophet in spite of his miserable shortcomings and utter failures was beyond a miracle. That God's Word could give new life and faith to a pagan city was an even greater miracle. There would be more Israelites like Jonah who would struggle with rebellion, pride, self-righteousness, and jealousy. There might be more cities like Nineveh—filled with wicked, idolatrous, and immoral people, but people with immortal souls loved by this very big God. Maybe some people someday could relate to Jonah's experiences if he could write them down. Surely the Word of the Lord would come to them too. They would find this God compassionate toward all sinners, toward them. One day they would look back on the sin-bearer whom God would send to Israel for the world.

The evening sun lowered in the sky. Jonah could see from the long shadows outside his tiny window that he didn't have long before it would be dark. He would work quickly and begin writing before nightfall. Perhaps the Lord could use him one more time.

How Does Jonah Remind Us of Jesus?

Within himself Jonah fought the pride and exclusivity that Jesus fought in the hearts of the Israelites of his day. Jesus warned his own disciples against jealously guarding his gift of forgiveness and eternal life instead of taking it to others. He told a parable about workers who were hired at various times during the day. They were all paid alike by their employer. Those hired first complained that those who worked less time got paid the same. The employer asked: "Don't I have the right to do what I want with my own money? Or are you envious because I am generous?" (Matthew 20:15). The problem of God's people being envious of others who are blessed by God's grace would endure throughout the New Testament.

Jesus' enemies, particularly the Pharisees and the teachers of the law, wanted miraculous proof that Jesus was the promised sin-deliverer. Jesus told them: "A wicked and adulterous generation asks for a miraculous sign! But none will be given it except the sign of the prophet Jonah. For as Jonah was three days and three nights in the belly of a huge fish, so the Son of Man will be three days and three nights in the heart of the earth. The men of Nineveh will stand up at the judgment with this generation and condemn it; for they repented at the preaching of Jonah, and now one greater than Jonah is here" (Matthew 12:39-41). Jesus was, of course, referring to his own resurrection from the dead on the third day—proof that he lived for all sinners and died for all sin: the Ninevites', the Israelites', Jonah's, and ours.